HIP-HOP & R&B

Culture, Music & Storytelling

HIP-HOP & R&B

Culture, Music & Storytelling

Beyoncé

Bruno Mars

Cardi B

Chance the Rapper

DJ Khaled

Drake

Jay-Z

Pharrell

Pitbull

Rihanna

The Weeknd

HIP-HOP & R&B

Drake

Culture, Music & Storytelling

Mason Crest
450 Parkway Drive, Suite D
Broomall, Pennsylvania 19008
(866) MCP-BOOK (toll free)

First printing
9 8 7 6 5 4 3 2 1

hardback: 978-1-4222-4180-6
series: 978-1-4222-4176-9
ebook: 978-1-4222-7622-8

Library of Congress Cataloging-in-Publication Data

Names: Snellgrove, Chris.
Title: Drake / Chris Snellgrove.
Description: Broomall, PA : Mason Crest, 2018. | Series: Hip-hop & R&B: culture, music & storytelling.
Identifiers: LCCN 2018020771 (print) | LCCN 2018022429 (ebook) | ISBN 9781422276228 (eBook) | ISBN 9781422241806 (hardback) | ISBN 9781422241769 (series)
Subjects: LCSH: Drake, 1986---Juvenile literature. | Rap musicians--Canada--Juvenile literature.
Classification: LCC ML3930.D73 (ebook) | LCC ML3930.D73 S64 2018 (print) | DDC 782.421649092 [B] --dc23
LC record available at https://lccn.loc.gov/2018020771

Developed and Produced by National Highlights, Inc.
Editor: Susan Uttendorfsky
Interior and cover design: Annalisa Gumbrecht, Studio Gumbrecht
Production: Michelle Luke

QR CODES AND LINKS TO THIRD-PARTY CONTENT

CONTENTS

KEY ICONS TO LOOK FOR:

Words to understand: These words with their easy-to-understand definitions will increase the reader's understanding of the text while building vocabulary skills.

Sidebars: This boxed material within the main text allows readers to build knowledge, gain insights, explore possibilities, and broaden their perspectives by weaving together additional information to provide realistic and holistic perspectives.

Educational videos: Readers can view videos by scanning our QR codes, providing them with additional educational content to supplement the text. Examples include news coverage, moments in history, speeches, iconic sports moments, and much more!

Text-dependent questions: These questions send the reader back to the text for more careful attention to the evidence presented there.

Research projects: Readers are pointed toward areas of further inquiry connected to each chapter. Suggestions are provided for projects that encourage deeper research and analysis.

Series of glossary of key terms: This back-of-the-book glossary contains terminology used throughout this series. Words found here increase the reader's ability to read and comprehend higher-level books and articles in this field.

Drive one

Chapter 1

Drake's Greatest Moments

Drake is one of a very small group of musicians (including breakout phenomenon Childish Gambino) who first achieved fame as an actor before becoming a successful musician. He starred in the teenage drama *Degrassi: The Next Generation* for a time, but in 2009, he left to pursue his dream of breaking into the musical industry.

While this may have been seen as a career gamble, it eventually paid off. After making a splash with three mixtapes, he signed on to Young Money Entertainment in 2009, which propelled him to worldwide fame.

Since then, Drake has been a musician with the Midas touch, turning everything he creates into gold. His albums have been wildly successful, and he has broken musical chart records and won multiple Grammy Awards. It's easy to look at this thriving career and imagine that everything came very easily to him. However, the stories of his early breakthroughs are filled with drama and suspense.

From Actor to Singer

Drake's big break did not come from his singing, but through his acting. He left high school to act as a high schooler in *Degrassi: The Next Generation*, and he starred on the show for seven years. Even as he built an international fan base, though, he was

Trey Songz at the 2010 MTV Video Music Awards

secretly plotting his musical career. When Degrassi's producers forced him to choose between a life onscreen and a life behind a microphone, Drake left the acting world behind forever.

He released three mixtapes before he was officially signed to a label. These mixtapes actually showcased Drake's creative shrewdness and business savvy very early on. For instance, he knew the value of making contacts with other artists. The first mixtape, Room for Improvement, also featured the talents of Lupe Fiasco and Trey Songz, two musicians who were more well-known at the time than Drake. This collaboration helped make the first mixtape a hit, and the success of his second mixtape, Comeback Season, landed his music video for *Replacement Girl*, featuring Trey Songz, on BET, massively increasing his exposure.

In those early years, Drake's mixtapes also served as a way for him to get noticed by the major movers and shakers in the music business. For instance, James "Jas" Prince, music CEO, recounts that the reason Drake first met Lil Wayne was because Prince played some of Drake's songs for him, including *Replacement Girl*. Wayne was so impressed that he invited Drake to hang out with him in Houston and brought Drake with him while he toured. As Prince recalls, there was a single moment when Wayne realized how famous Drake was: He heard "15,000 people" all yelling "Jimmy!"—the name of Drake's *Degrassi* character.

Lil Wayne knew he had the full package in Drake: A up-and-coming music sensation who could sing remixes as well as original music, and he was already famous. There was a well-publicized bidding war when the time came to sign Drake, but it was no real surprise that Lil Wayne's company, Young Money Entertainment, snagged him. This was the beginning of Drake's journey into international megafame, and the next time he joined Lil Wayne on a tour, they were both the stars of the show!

Lil Wayne

Breakout Success

Drake had already achieved a very different kind of success by performing in the popular teenage drama *Degrassi: The Next Generation*. He starred in the show for seven seasons, playing the character of James Brooks. There was a bit of irony in the role, as the James character was forced to change his focus from basketball success to music, where he eventually achieved fame and recognition.

It turned out that Drake was in between careers in real life too, juggling his musical aspirations and his acting duties. In an interview with *W* (magazine), he described being "kicked off the show" in 2009 when its creators forced him to choose between music and acting.

Mixtapes

Room for Improvement

(Released February 14, 2006)

By the standards of his future success, the accomplishments of Drake's first mixtape were very humble, selling only 6,000 copies in 2006. Still, it helped establish Drake as a musician and built up an audience for his next mixtape.

One of the most impressive songs from this first mixtape is *Make Things Right,* in which Drake emphasizes that there is more to life than fame and fortune.

Scan the code to listen to *Make Things Right*, a hit song from Drake's first mixtape

Collaborations

- *Money (Remix)*, featuring Nickelus F
- *AM 2 PM*, featuring Nickelus F
- *Bad Meaning Good*, featuring Slakah the Beatchild
- *Make Things Right,* featuring Slakah the Beatchild
- *A Scorpio's Mind*, featuring Nickelus F
- *S.T.R.E.S.S.*, featuring Nickelus F
- *Kick, Push (Remix)* by Lupe Fiasco, featuring Drake

Comeback Season

(Released September 01, 2007)

When Drake released his sophomore mixtape, it brought him even greater exposure. He created a music video for *Replacement Girl*, a collaboration with Trey Songz, that was featured on BET. The appearance was a first for any unsigned Canadian musician.

In many ways, *Replacement Girl* put Drake on the map.

Collaborations

- *Closer*, featuring Andreena Mill
- *Replacement Girl,* featuring Trey Songz
- *Give Ya*, featuring Trey Songz
- *Don't U Have a Man*, featuring Dwele and Little Brother
- *The Last Hope*, featuring Kardinal Offishall and Andreena Mill
- *Must Hate Money*, featuring Rich Boy
- *Do What U Do (Remix)*, featuring Malice and Nickelus F
- *Easy to Please*, featuring Richie Sosa
- *Faded*, featuring Nickelus F
- *Underdog*, featuring Trey Songz
- *Think Good Thoughts*, featuring Phonte and eLZhi
- *Man of the Year*, featuring Lil Wayne

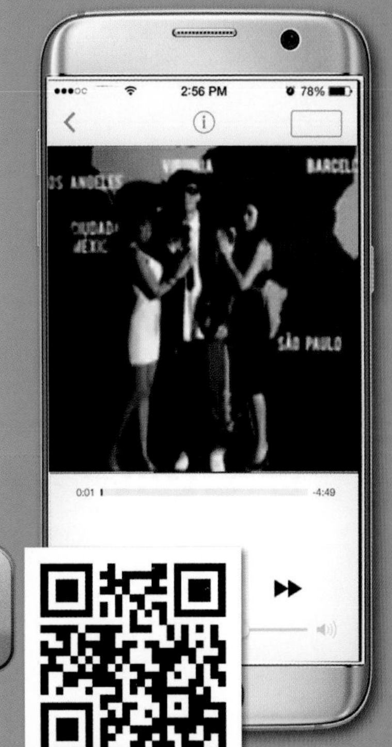

Scan the code to join 20 million other viewers who have watched the music video for *Replacement Girl*

So Far Gone
(Released February 13, 2009)

Drake kept the momentum up by releasing So Far Gone in 2009—his golden ticket to worldwide fame. Two of its singles became hits on the *Billboard* Hot 100 list: *Best I Ever Had* was number two, and *Successful* reached number seventeen. The mixtape received almost universal acclaim from critics around the world.

The success led to Drake's signing with Young Money Entertainment in 2009. This launched him into worldwide fame, including a series of successful albums and tours. Its achievements also led to his departure from *Degrassi: The Next Generation*.

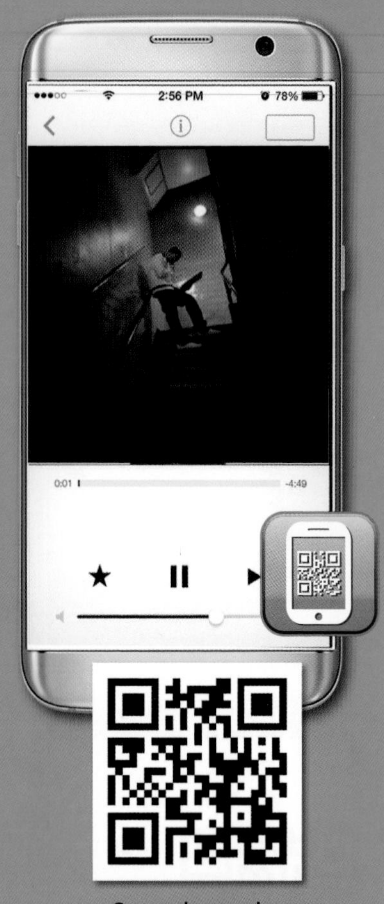

Scan the code to watch the music video for Drake's smash song *Best I Ever Had*

Collaborations

- *Successful*, featuring Trey Songz and Lil Wayne
- *Let's Call It Off*, featuring Peter Bjorn and John
- *Ignorant S*, featuring Lil Wayne
- *A Night Off*, featuring Lloyd
- *Little Bit*, featuring Lykke Li
- *Unstoppable (Remix)*, featuring Santigold and Lil Wayne
- *Uptown*, featuring Bun B and Lil Wayne
- *Bria's Interlude*, featuring Omarion

Albums

Thank Me Later

(Released June 15, 2010)

In 2010, Drake released his first real album as part of the Young Money Entertainment label. This debut creation became a critical and commercial hit. The first single, *Over*, reached number fourteen on the *Billboard* Hot 100 Chart, and the second single, *Find Your Love*, peaked at number five. The album led to multiple Grammy Award nominations, including Best Rap Album and Best New Artist for Drake himself. As of 2016, the album had sold over 5 million copies worldwide.

Collaborations

- *Fireworks*, featuring Alicia Keys
- *Up All Night*, featuring Nicki Minaj
- *Fancy*, featuring T.I. and Swizz Beatz
- *Shut It Down*, featuring The Dream
- *Unforgettable*, featuring Young Jeezy
- *Light Up*, featuring Jay-Z
- *Miss Me*, featuring Lil Wayne

Take Care

(Released November 15, 2011)

Drake's second album, Take Care, was a more mature effort, and it debuted in November of 2011. The singer claimed he felt rushed on his first album, and he wanted to "take care" and take his time on the newest work. Audiences certainly enjoyed the effort. Singles scored hits, such as *Headlines*, peaking at number thirteen on the *Billboard* Hot 100, and the second single, *Make Me Proud*, reaching ninety-seven.

Once again nominated for multiple Grammy Awards, he won the 2013 Grammy Award for Best Rap Album. While it did not sell as well as his first album, Take Care sold a little over 3 million copies

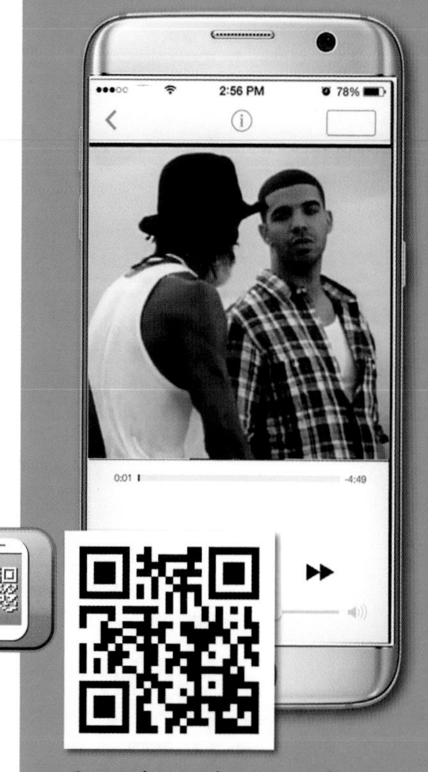

Scan the code to watch the music video for *Find Your Love* from Drake's first studio album

worldwide, and the album was certified quadruple Platinum by the RIAA (Recording Industry Association of America).

Scan the code to listen to the standout song *Headlines* from Drake's second studio album

Collaborations

- *Crew Love*, featuring The Weeknd
- *Take Care*, featuring Rihanna
- *Buried Alive Interlude*, featuring Kendrick Lamar
- *We'll Be Fine*, featuring Birdman
- *Make Me Proud*, featuring Nicki Minaj
- *Lord Knows*, featuring Rick Ross
- *The Real Her*, featuring Lil Wayne and André 3000
- *HYFR*, featuring Lil Wayne

Nothing Was the Same

(Released September 24, 2013)

His third album had a very ambitious name: Nothing Was the Same. The second single from this successful effort, *Hold On, We're Going Home*, topped the *Billboard* Hot 100 Chart. The album itself debuted at number one on the *Billboard* Top 200 Chart.

While it did not result in any wins, Drake was again nominated for multiple Grammy Awards for this album, and it sold over 2 million copies worldwide. It has been certified triple Platinum by RIAA, and also brought us the song that could well be Drake's theme song: *Started from the Bottom*, a song that playfully highlights and celebrates Drake's meteoric rise to superstar status.

Collaborations

- *From Time*, featuring Jhené Aiko
- *Hold On, We're Going Home*, featuring Majid Jordan
- *Pound Cake/Paris Morton Music 2*, featuring Jay-Z
- *All Me*, featuring 2 Chainz and Big Sean (only available on the deluxe edition of Nothing was the same)

Views
(Released April 29, 2016)

From a pure sales standpoint, previous album releases made it look like Drake was sleeping. Each sold fewer copies than the one before! But this changed with his fourth album, Views. The singles from the album were very successful. *One Dance* became Spotify's most-streamed song of all time in October of 2016, and that same song was Drake's first number one single in his home country of Canada. The album sales were phenomenal. As of 2016, the album had sold over 5 million copies worldwide, effectively matching the popularity and star power of his runaway debut album.

Scan the code to see the official music video for *Hold On, We're Going Home*

Noteworthy Collaborations

While Drake has certainly made it to the top, he had some help every now and then. In fact, some his best, most award-winning creations were in collaboration with other artists.

With You

by Lil Wayne, featuring Drake
(Released September 27, 2010)

This song is primarily hip-hop in nature, and it was released as part of Lil Wayne's eighth studio album, I Am Not a Human Being. Lyrically, the song is a clear mix of Wayne's and Drake's influences. The song is about a couple's relationship, and it combines Lil Wayne's bawdier style with Drake's more typical romantic thoughts.

What's My Name?

by Rihanna, featuring Drake
(Released October 26, 2010)

This song has an electric, R&B sound and was part of Rihanna's album Loud. The song focuses primarily on the relationship between a man and a woman, represented by Drake and Rihanna, respectively. They also portray these characters in a music video for the song. The song eventually reached number two on *Billboard*'s Hot R&B/Hip-Hop Songs Chart.

Moment 4 Life

by Nicki Minaj, featuring Drake
(Released December 07, 2010)

This traditional rap song was released as part of Nicki Minaj's debut album, PINK FRIDAY. The song was inspired by Minaj's childhood dream of becoming a famous rap star with her friend. Drake, whose own career was starting to take off, essentially lived out the fantasy with her. And it worked! This song, along with the rest of the album, put Nicki Minaj on the map.

PROBLEMS

by A$AP Rocky, featuring Drake,
2 Chainz, and Kendrick Lamar
(Released October 24, 2012)

This award-winning single was the second release from A$AP Rocky's debut album, LONG. LIVE. ASAP. The song reached number two on *Billboard*'s Hot R&B/Hip-Hop Songs, Hot Rap Songs, and U.S. Rhythmic charts, and was certified triple Platinum by the RIAA. It also reached number twenty-one on Complex's list of 2012's Fifty Best Songs.

The song was performed live at the 2013 BET Award show and won Best Collaboration.

Kendrick Lamar at the 2017 MTV Video Music Awards held at the Forum in Inglewood, CA,s on August 27, 2017

CABARET

by Justin Timberlake, featuring Drake
(Released September 27, 2013)

Justin Timberlake and Drake are like two great tastes that taste great together. They proved that by collaborating on CABARET, a pop-infused soul song by Timberlake that Drake added some great rapping to. The song was very successful, hitting the eighteenth spot on the *Billboard*'s U.S. R&B Songs Chart.

Scan the code to watch Drake perform *One Dance* on *Saturday Night Live*

MINE

by Beyoncé, featuring Drake

(Released December 13, 2013)

This R&B song blends in elements of hip-hop and rap. It was released by Beyoncé as part of her fifth studio album, BEYONCÉ. The song featured Drake, and while not all critics appreciated his contribution, his collaboration with such a notable artist illustrated his own rising fame.

WORK

by Rihanna, featuring Drake

(Released January 27, 2016)

The Jamaican dancehall lead single from Rihanna's eighth studio album, ANTI, reached number one on *Billboard*'s Hot 100 singles chart within 36 hours of its release on iTunes. *Work*'s theme is a woman who is seeking a deep, meaningful connection with a man (Drake) who is only interested in sex.

At the 2016 American Music Awards, *Work* won Favorite Soul/R&B Song, and it won the BET Best Collaboration award for the same year. It also won the iHeartRadio Music Awards Best Collaboration song and R&B Song of the Year for 2017. In an interview with *Vogue*, Rihanna had this to say about Drake:

> *"Drake has a lot to offer. He's very intelligent, and so I trust him a lot with his direction. Doing a collaboration with him, you know it's going to be great. Everything he does is so amazing. He's so talented that you kind of just trust that it'll be right. And plus, we know each other, so I know that whatever he writes is going to be honest, and it's going to make sense to where I'm at in my life. That's the difference. We know each other."*

Major Tours

In order to meet his fans, build his brand, and extend his legend, Drake has gone on tour many times. Here are the major tours he has been on.

Away from Home Tour

This aptly named tour, Drake's first, began on April 05 and ended on November 06, 2010. The tour took the Canadian singer through much of Canada and the United States, with Drake performing in a variety of locations that included the UCF Arena in Florida, the Memorial Coliseum in Kentucky, and the Comcast Center in Massachusetts.

Club Paradise Tour

Drake's second major tour ran from February 14 to June 17, 2012. The Club Paradise Tour marked Drake's growing success, and he brought fellow musicians Kendrick Lamar and A$AP Rocky along as he visited cities in both Canada and the United States, as well as locations throughout all of Europe. The major stops included the Sprint Center in Kansas City, the Manchester Arena in England, and the Heineken Music Hall in the Netherlands.

Overall, he made sixty-four stops on this tour and included a number of surprise musician cameos, like Wacka Flocka Flame, 2 Chainz, and Meek Mill.

Would You Like a Tour?

Drake's third major tour was also his longest running. Would You Like a Tour? lasted from October 18, 2013, to March 05, 2015. Gaps in this long tour allowed the singer to work on new projects and, in some cases, even participate in other tours.

It was also Drake's most ambitious tour to date, taking the singer throughout Canada, the United States, and a variety of locations in Europe. He visited more of the world than he ever had before on tour along the sixty-six stops, including New Zealand and Australia! Musician Future toured along with him, and there were also appearances by musicians PartyNextDoor and The Weeknd.

Drake vs. Lil Wayne

In many ways, this was Drake's weirdest tour. It ran from August 08 to September 27, 2014, and was sponsored by Capcom, the makers of the popular *Street Fighter* series of video games. Both singers performed at each concert, and a special app allowed attendees to determine things like who would perform first and who the winner of the "fight" was. During this short tour, the singers only visited venues in the United States, including the Hollywood Bowl in Los Angeles, California, and the Red Rocks Amphitheatre in Colorado.

Summer Sixteen Tour

Drake's next concert tour launched in 2016,

and it was appropriately named the Summer Sixteen Tour. It ran from July 20 to October 08, 2016. This circuit was a return to Drake's roots, as he concentrated on visiting cities in Canada and the United States. The fifty-four shows included visits to the Frank Irwin Music Center in Austin, Texas, and the Verizon Center in Washington, DC. One notable feature of this concert was that Drake toured with fellow musician Future.

Boy Meets World Tour

As of this writing, Drake's most recent tour was the Boy Meets World Tour. It ran from January 18 to November 20, 2017. Its forty-three stops spanned locations such as the Spark Arena in Auckland, New Zealand, and the Mercedes-Benz Arena in Berlin, Germany.

While the name of the tour was an amusing homage to the popular television show *Boy Meets World*, the name of this tour was quite literal. Drake actually had no stops in Canada or the United States during this tour, instead focusing on visiting locations in Europe and Oceania.

The Uncertain Road

Drake's path so far has taken him into the stratosphere, achieving wealth, fame, and an absolutely elite entertainer status. However, he did not complete this journey overnight. Before the world could get to know just how awesome Drake is, he had to complete his very own road to the top.

Words to Understand

hallmark: a real or symbolic marker indicating that a person or object has met a certain standard of quality.

prestigious: full of great prestige; a person who is an object of other people's honor and affection.

leverage: to use something (such as a particular circumstance or opportunity) to achieve the best possible advantage or situation.

Chapter 2

Drake's Road to the Top

Using What He Experienced

One **hallmark** of hip-hop and rap artists is that they sing about their own lives. Therefore, fans expect a certain level of over-the-top drama and extraordinary circumstances. However, even by the industry's standards, Drake lived through a lot in his first three decades on Earth. Most people will never experience so much in their whole lifetime! This extraordinary journey, though, began with some very humble steps.

Before Drake could revolutionize the world of singing, he had to navigate the complex world of his parents' divorce. Afterward, he had to reconcile the different faiths of his parents and develop both a spiritual and cultural identity that is uniquely his own. And Drake first pursued the world of acting—performing a major role in an iconic television show that lasted for seven years—before he decided to focus on singing.

Many fans were surprised by Drake's "new" focus on music, but many of them didn't realize that music has been in Drake's DNA from the very beginning!

Family Background

Drake was born on October 24, 1986, with the full name Aubrey Drake Graham. He is the only son of Dennis Graham and his mother, Sandi Graham. As far as the world knows, Drake has no brothers or sisters, though he has confused some of his fans by casually mentioning a "sis." No woman has been identified as his sister, however.

His parents played an important role in shaping both his identity and his future career. For instance, Drake was born into a very musical family—his father played the drums for famous rock star Jerry Lee Lewis, while his uncle was a bassist for the band Sly and the Family Stone. While his mother was not herself a musician, Drake likes to recount that Sandi's mom (his grandmother) babysat for Aretha Franklin.

A wax figure of singer/songwriter Jerry Lee Lewis at Madame Tussauds in New York City

Unfortunately, his parents divorced when Drake was five, and he was raised by his mother. Her religious upbringing was influential to his early life. Dennis Graham is Catholic and Sandi Graham is Jewish, so Drake had a very traditional Jewish upbringing, including celebrating his Bar Mitzvah at the age of thirteen and observing High Holy Days. This religious focus also shaped his early educational experiences.

Education

From the time Drake began living with his mother at the age of five, he was raised in two different parts of Canada: First, he lived off Weston Road, a relatively rough area. They moved to the more affluent Forest Hill area when he was in sixth grade, and this created a childhood tension between his more humble background and the wealthy background of his peers. His elementary education was conducted in the Forest Hill Public School, which he attended through eighth grade. Then his high school education began at Forest Hill Collegiate Institute.

The school itself is **prestigious**, but Drake felt isolated—he was a poor African-American Jewish child in a rich school predominately attended by white students, and he believed that most of his peers couldn't fully understand his life experiences. However, at least one classmate understood his potential. This classmate's father is an agent for actors, and the son recommended that Drake audition. The father became his agent and helped him land a role on *Degrassi: The Next*

Generation. After he got the spot, Drake dropped out of school in 2001 at the age of fifteen.

However, getting his high school diploma became important, so in 2012, he returned to school at the Vaughan Road Academy and completed the necessary exams. He was twenty-six years old by that time and had already achieved wealth and worldwide fame, but he still described graduating high school as "one of the greatest feelings in my entire life."

The *Degrassi* Years

As described, Drake auditioned for and landed the role of Jimmy Brooks on *Degrassi: The Next Generation*, but it wasn't easy. To hear Drake recount the tale, the producing company's process of casting the character of Jimmy Brooks and other roles had taken the better part of a year, and Drake auditioned in the final weeks of casting.

This television series was a spinoff of the *Degrassi* franchise of TV shows that focused on the lives of different teenagers at different stages of their lives. *The Next Generation* was the fourth show within this franchise, and it focused on the lives of teenagers attending Degrassi Community School. Drake's character was an aspiring basketball player whose hoop dreams were cut short when he was shot and crippled by a classmate. When he had to use a wheelchair for the rest of the series, Drake's character turned to music as an outlet for self-expression. Ironically enough, Drake himself was doing the same thing while filming the show!

Previously, Drake had not shown much interest in anything like formal music training. While in school, he was more interested in acting than music. However, he began creating mixtapes on the side while working on the hit series, and the arrangement finally proved impossible to maintain.

Watch a scene from *Degrassi* where Jimmy gets shot

At first, Drake tried to juggle both his acting "day job" and his musical career, but the late nights and constant work took a toll on his acting performance. Drake recalls staying up to record music until 4:00 or 5:00 a.m. and then starting a full day of filming at 9:00 a.m. Eventually, the producers of *Degrassi* gave him an ultimatum, forcing him to choose between continuing his acting profession and pursuing his burgeoning musical career. Obviously, Drake chose to follow his heart into music, and it was this simple choice that eventually made him a household name.

Fast Fact 1:

Drake's popularity from his time on *Degrassi* helped launch his music career. Jas Prince, a music producer traveling with Lil Wayne on tour, later recounted a story of a concert with 15,000 people in attendance. Once the crowd heard that Drake was there, they began shouting "Jimmy!" (the name of his character) in hopes of seeing him play.

First Album Debut

Drake produced a series of successful mixtapes before the debut of his first studio album, THANK ME LATER, on June 15, 2010. Those mixtapes created very high expectations for the album, as Drake received two Grammy nominations (Best Rap Solo Performance and Best Rap Song) for one song from that final SO FAR GONE mixtape—*Best I Ever Had*. His high profile from those nominations, as well as his increasing worldwide recognition, made him a hot commodity. Multiple studios made enticing offers, but he decided to sign with Young Money Entertainment, Lil Wayne's label. This occurred after Wayne invited Drake to visit him in Houston and then to travel with him.

Drake's contract was quite generous. They paid the young singer an advance of $2 million, and Drake got to keep his publishing rights. Even better, he pays a relatively low 25 percent of his income to the company. The label's clout, combined with his rising fame, ensured securing some sizzling guest stars on that debut album. The list of high-profile musical stars included Nicki Minaj and Kanye West.

Drake's admirers were in great anticipation for the album, as buzz had been building around him for years thanks to his successful mixtapes, creative music videos, and unexpected Grammy nominations. Those fans bought the album in droves, with it selling almost half a million copies in the first week and debuting at the top spot on the *Billboard* Top 200 Chart. All of the singles released from this album landed within the top forty songs on the *Billboard* Hot 100 singles chart.

The album was just as much of a hit with critics as it was with fans. Many publications listed Thank Me Later as one of the top albums of the year. This included *Rolling Stone*, which ranked it as the seventh best album of the year, and *Time* (magazine), which bumped it up to fifth.

Overall, the album was well-liked across the board, and while some critics felt that Drake had not fully matured yet—as either man or musician—the album represented an amazing commercial and critical success for this musician on the rise.

Fast Fact 2:

It is very likely that Drake's growing relationship with Lil Wayne contributed toward him joining Young Money Entertainment, Lil Wayne's label. In the wake of Drake's great success with his third mixtape, So Far Gone, many labels competed to sign him, including Universal Motown and Atlantic Records. Prior to this, however, Drake had spent a lot of time with Lil Wayne both socially and professionally (they had recorded songs together, including *Ransom* and *I Want This Forever*). Signing with Young Money Entertainment allowed them to easily collaborate in the future, including their Drake vs. Lil Wayne Tour.

Final Thoughts

Every successful music artist has their own distinctive journey to the top. Some aspects of Drake's story are more familiar than others—for instance, the influence of parents encouraged the musical expression

BET AWARDS 11
Ford
Drive one.

of many future stars, including major names like Bruno Mars. Other aspects of Drake's story, though, are completely unique to his own life. His many years of acting on *Degrassi* meant that Drake had a built-in audience, and he was already a familiar face known to fans around the world long before he distributed his first mixtape.

Drake's skill regarding his mixtapes was particularly impressive. While he may have "only" been a high school dropout at the time, he was able to expertly market each new mixtape and then turn around and **leverage** that fame into superstardom. Receiving Grammy Award nominations on a song from a mixtape is insanely impressive, and it is not a surprise that Drake had multiple studios making offers to sign him.

Soon Drake would be a dominant force in the musical world, achieving greater sales and endorsements that spread his fame farther and wider.

Text-Dependent Questions:

1. What is Drake's full name?
2. What physical format did Drake release music on before he was signed to any label?
3. What unfinished work did Drake complete in 2012?

Research Project:

Describe a mixtape you would like to create to impress your friends and family. Name at least ten songs that would be on this mixtape, and explain briefly what the significance of each of these songs is.

Words to Understand

ambient:
a musical style that relies on electronic sounds, gentle music, and the lack of a regular beat to create a relaxed mood for the listener.

introspective:
someone who analyzes their own words and actions; contemplative and thoughtful.

venture:
a risky opportunity; the word is meant to evoke a sense of adventure.

Chapter 3

On Top of the World

Success Through Sales

The bottom line for any professional musician is just how well their music moves around the world. Fortunately, this is an area that Drake excels at. In fact, a quick glance at the numbers for his albums illustrates this artist has nonstop staying power—and some of the most loyal fans in the business.

Drake's Album Achievements

Thank Me Later

(Released June 15, 2010)

After a series of three successful mixtapes and becoming more popular on the global stage, Thank Me Later was Drake's opportunity to reach additional fans in new places. This first studio album established him as a singer who can reflect on his life with humor and insight through a variety of musical styles. He brought **ambient** sound and synthetic groove to the rap game, and he seemed just as happy to make fun of himself as he was to spill the secrets of the rap world via his confessional album. Despite leaking out online two weeks early, Thank Me Later was an instant success, debuting at number one on *Billboard*'s Top 200 list.

The critical and public response to this album was striking. Reviewers praised Drake's introspection and his accessibility, and it seemed people simply could not get enough of his music. The album sold over 4.5 million copies in the United States alone by 2016, and worldwide, sold almost 400,000 more in the same time frame. In the United States, sales reached nearly half a million copies within one week of its release, which was doubly impressive considering that the album was leaked online before its official release. The album was certified Platinum by the RIAA, and this success proved to be a good omen for Drake's future work.

Swizz Beatz

One of the notable collaborations on this album was *Fancy*, featuring T.I. and Swizz Beatz. This song became number one on *Billboard*'s U.S. Rap Songs Chart and number twenty-five on *Billboard*'s Hot 100.

Take Care

(Released November 15, 2011)

Drake's sophomore release came nearly a year and a half after his first album debuted. From an artistic standpoint, he did not deviate much from the form he established in Thank Me Later. Take Care demonstrated he was still the same **introspective** rapper who approached topics with humor, emotion, and genuine thoughtfulness.

Scan the code to watch Drake talk about the making of Thank Me Later, his first studio album

In terms of marketing this work, Drake wasn't afraid to lean on his famous friends. The album was promoted through the release of eight different singles, and these included collaborations with Rihanna, Nicki Minaj, Lil Wayne, The Weeknd, and Rick Ross.

The collaboration with Rihanna, *Make Me Proud*, is an especially moving song. Another collaboration on this album had a very unique sound—*Crew Love*, featuring The Weeknd. It blended The Weeknd's smooth R&B sound with a bit of hip-hop from Drake, creating something emotionally moving and quite catchy. The collaborations helped

Take Care follow the success of Drake's first album, with it debuting at the top spot on *Billboard*'s Top 200 Chart.

Critically, the album was another hit. Commentators noted that his talent had grown, and the songs stretched the boundaries of what rap and hip-hop were capable of, along with Drake's own limits. Audiences were in agreement with the critics, with strong sales. By 2016, it had sold nearly 2.5 million copies in the United States alone, and over half a million additional copies worldwide. Audiences everywhere streamed much of the album, which helped it become RIAA-certified as quadruple Platinum.

Scan the code to watch a great interview with Drake about the making of Take Care

All of this success placed extra pressure on Drake to succeed, with critics and the public alike wondering if he could sustain this level of quality for a third album.

Nothing Was the Same
(Released September 24, 2013)

Almost two years passed before Drake dropped his third album, Nothing Was the Same. Despite the fairly dramatic title, the effort represented more of the same. Once again, he blended honest explorations and assessments of his own life and, once again, critics praised improvements in his composition and craft.

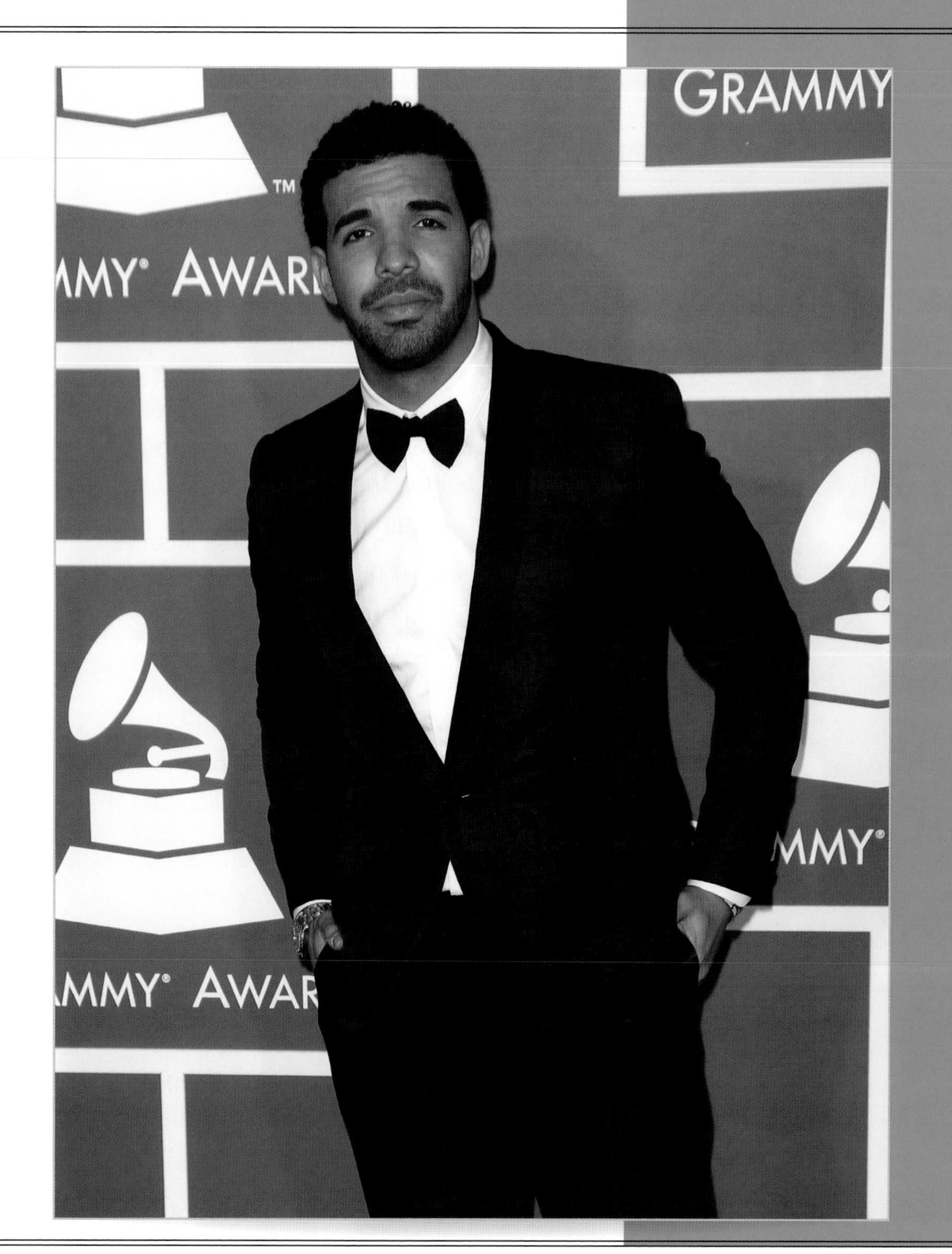
GRAMMY

Hip-Hop recording artist Tauheed Epps, aka 2 Chainz

Another similarity to TAKE CARE was how aggressively he marketed it. Drake released seven singles from this album, and they included more from his famous friends, such as 2 Chainz and Big Sean.

Despite the album's title, one other thing certainly was the same—like Drake's previous two albums, this one debuted at number one on the prestigious *Billboard* Top 200 Chart.

NOTHING WAS THE SAME was well-received by critics, who noted the expert transitions within the songs as well as the emotional depths Drake mined out of his own life. Fans loved it as well, purchasing nearly 2 million copies in the United States alone and nearly half a million copies worldwide. The availability of streaming content increased Drake's visibility and popularity, and the album was certified triple Platinum by the RIAA.

Views
(Released April 29, 2016)

As of 2017, Views is Drake's most recent album. While all of his previous releases were critical and commercial successes, it was tough to ignore that each album sold fewer copies than the one before it. Views changed that trend. Drake focused on the kinds of songs his audiences loved, including five more collaborations with well-known music artists like Rihanna, Kanye West, and Jay-Z.

Scan the code to watch Drake discuss Nothing Was the Same, as well as what it's like to work alongside some of the world's most famous musicians

The result was an album that failed to move many of Drake's critics but still sold an impressive amount of copies. One of the notable collaborations is *Too Good*, featuring Rihanna. This song landed on the thirty-second spot on *Billboard*'s list of 100 Best Pop Songs for 2016, showcasing Drake's versatility.

Conceptually, the album was about changing the views we have of certain things, but

Scan the code to watch Drake talk about the making of *Views*, his fourth album, as well as life in the record business

Drake's results didn't change much. Like the previous three releases, this one debuted at the very top of the *Billboard* 200 Chart.

While not a dud, *Views* was awarded a lower score on Metacritic (a website that creates an aggregate tally for albums based on the opinions of various professional critics) than any of Drake's other albums. Reviewers noted that he was no longer stretching himself as an artist and had instead settled into a comfy routine. But fans had no objections! The quadruple Platinum album sold over 4.5 million copies in the United States alone. Its commercial success demonstrated that Drake was more popular than ever before.

Capitalizing on Drake's Popularity with Endorsements

When an artist achieves such consistent popular success, it is natural that companies want to hire that artist to promote their products. It's a win-win situation for both parties, as more people are exposed to the music performer and hopefully the manufacturer sells more product!

Sprite

One of Drake's first major endorsements was of Sprite, a popular brand of soda manufactured by The Coca-Cola Company. In early 2010, before the debut of his first studio album, it was announced that they would be working on the Sprite Spark campaign. Drake himself was passionate about the project because, as he said,

> *The campaign is really about creativity through music and film and promotes fresh thinking and originality. I guess they recognized my potential based off what has happened with my music career in the last year. I think it's a great thing to be responsible, in a way, for exciting young kids.*

His first commercial for Sprite focused on the struggle of perfecting and producing a song to match the creative vision in his head. He went on to work with Sprite on many other **ventures** that year, including judging an NBA Slam Dunk Showdown and a Step-Off Dance Competition. These resulted in Sprite awarding $1.5 million in scholarships.

Fast Fact 3:

Drake's commercial for Sprite is very earnest, as he was young and his career was just beginning. Getting all of his songs just right was crucial in order to build his brand and launch a successful career. He said as much in an interview with *Billboard*: "It happens all the time—it's the beautiful struggle…" He described how the commercial represents his own process.

> *"For an artist who's a perfectionist...you may sit there for twenty minutes or three days writing." The commercial was also personal for Drake because he brought along Noah "40" Shebib, a Canadian record producer, and Boi-1da, two colleagues critical to his creative process.*

Nike

Watch Drake's first Sprite commercial here

A major sign that an artist has become a big deal is when they become a brand unto themselves. Sometimes, for instance, fans don't just want to hear their favorite singers—they want to wear them! That is certainly the case when it comes to Drake's ongoing collaboration with Nike.

On December 12, 2013, Drake announced that he would be working with Nike and Michael Jordan to design some of their famous Air Jordan shoes, which remain popular year after year. Drake was apparently very satisfied with the collaboration. In May of 2017, he met with several bigwigs at Nike's headquarters. While their exact plans haven't been unveiled yet, it looks like Nike just doesn't want to let Drake go.

This endorsement is symbolic as well, as Drake took over designing for Nike in 2013 right after Kanye West left, which illustrates Drake's ability to be a tastemaker in the worlds of both hip-hop and fashion.

Virginia Black

While Drake was already insanely successful in the music and fashion worlds, the hip-hop mogul decided that wasn't enough. That's why he teamed up with Brent Hocking, a former financier in the world of alcoholic beverages, to create a luxury whiskey named Virginia Black.

Drake was wise to collaborate with Hocking, who had previously designed other drink brands and sold them to such powerful figures as George Clooney and Sean "Diddy" Combs. When the brand was unveiled in 2016, it sold over 30,000 cases in its first year. Since then, Virginia Black has become a runaway success in the world of social media.

Scan the code to watch Drake describe what it's like to be part of Team Jordan

This early success may open the door for Drake to create more products that extend beyond music and fashion. The advertising has also given Drake yet another fun nickname—in the commercials, he calls himself the "Realest Dude Ever."

Apple Music

A sure sign of Drake's business savvy is that he recognized the rising popularity of streaming music and acted accordingly, teaming

Scan the code to watch one of Drake's funny commercials for Apple Music

up with Apple Music when it launched in 2015. Through this venue, Drake has released exclusive music and allowed his fans to stream his classics. He has also released some of his music exclusively through *Beats 1*, an Apple-owned online radio station that never stops broadcasting.

While releasing music digitally in a digital age may seem like a no-brainer, Drake once again proved what a tastemaker he is. Previously, he released his singles primarily through SoundCloud. Because Drake decided to switch to Apple, they have been able to compete with larger services, like Spotify, while SoundCloud has sunk into millions of dollars in debt, thanks in part to the absence of Drake. For Apple, his presence has been so successful that *Beats 1* DJ Zane Lowe has described Drake's live streams as "cultural moments."

Airbnb

Unlike other endorsements on this list, Drake does not currently have a formal agreement with Airbnb. Instead, they seem to enjoy a kind of a public-relations arrangement. Airbnb gifted Drake several nights in a lavish Los Angeles home that normally rents for a staggering $10,000 a night. In turn, Drake gave the company a shout-out on his Instagram account on April 24, 2017, and described the experience in glowing terms.

Only time will tell if this remains a temporary arrangement—with Drake helping to repair the company's image—or if it blossoms into its own separate deal.

Fast Fact 4:

Some cynical criticizers believe that Airbnb only reached out to Drake only because of a recent controversy about Airbnb hosts refusing guests on the basis of their race and/or ethnicity. The original incident occurred in February 2017, when an Airbnb host canceled a guest reservation at the last moment because, as he texted, she was "Asian." This kicked off much online discussion about how overwhelmingly white most of the Airbnb community is. In response, Airbnb has collaborated with the NAACP to try to foster more racial diversity among its hosts and guests. Because of this, some people think the timing of Drake's stay was not coincidental, and was meant to subtly highlight Airbnb's efforts to be more racially diverse and inclusive.

MatchaBar

In some ways, MatchaBar is one of Drake's most confusing endorsements. The company specializes in creating energy drinks made from caffeinated green tea powder and selling them via a trendy little cafe in New York City. However, they want to bottle their drink and sell it as a healthier alternative to soda and coffee. The company had been looking for investors, but no one could have predicted that Drake would invest in August of 2017. Obviously, the music superstar believes in the company's tagline, "Good things come to those who hustle." With his investment, they are on track to begin bottling and selling their green tea drinks in late 2017.

Major Awards Overview

American Music Awards

Favorite Rap/Hip-Hop Artist | Won in 2016

Favorite Rap/Hip-Hop Album—Views | Won in 2016

Favorite Soul/R&B Song—
Work, featuring Rihanna | Won in 2016

Favorite Rap/Hip-Hop Song—*Hotline Bling* | Won in 2016

BET Awards

Best Male Hip-Hop Artist | Won in 2010 and 2012

Best Group—Young Money Entertainment | Won in 2010

Best Collaboration—*Problems,* featuring A$AP Rocky, 2 Chainz, and Kendrick Lamar | Won in 2013

Video of the Year—*Started from the Bottom* | Won in 2013

Coca-Cola Viewers' Choice—*Started from the Bottom* | Won in 2013

Best Group—Young Money Entertainment | Won in 2014

Best Male Hip-Hop Artist | Won in 2014 and 2016

Coca-Cola Viewers' Choice—*Only*, featuring Nicki Minaj, Chris Brown, and Lil Wayne | Won in 2015

Best Collaboration—*Work*, featuring Rihanna | Won in 2016

Best Group—Drake and Future | Won in 2016

Billboard Music Awards

Top Rap Artist | Won in 2016 and 2017

Top Artist | Won in 2017

Top Hot 100 Artist | Won in 2017

Top Male Artist | Won in 2017

Top Billboard 200 Artist | Won in 2017

Top Song Sales Artist | Won in 2017

Top Streaming Songs Artist | Won in 2017

Top Billboard 200 Album—Views | Won in 2017

Top Rap Album—Views | Won in 2017

Top Streaming Song, Audio— *One Dance*, featuring Wizkid and Kyla | Won in 2017

Top Rap Tour | Won in 2017

BRIT Awards

International Male Solo Artist | Won in 2016

Grammy Awards

Best Rap Album—Take Care | Won in 2013

Best Rap/Sung Performance—*Hotline Bling* | Won in 2017

Best Rap Song—*Hotline Bling* | Won in 2017

MTV Video Music Awards

Best Hip-Hop Video—*HYFR*, featuring Lil Wayne | Won in 2012

Best Hip-Hop Video—*Hold On, We're Going Home,*
featuring Majid Jordan | Won in 2014

Best Hip-Hop Video—*Hotline Bling* | Won in 2016

Drake and Organik

A Rising Star

Drake is an artist who has continued to grow in every way. Creatively, he has tested the waters with new sounds, and as a businessman, he has taken on a variety of endorsements while making successful investments. Ultimately, all of this has served to increase Drake's worldwide popularity, and all of it is part of his long-term plan for building his own particular brand.

Text-Dependent Questions:

1. What label did Drake release his first official album through?
2. Which Drake album did music critics like the least?
3. What major soft drink brand has Drake endorsed?

Research Project:

Research the companies that have endorsed Drake. Now, write a 500-word paper explaining which of these companies you think has most helped Drake's brand and which company you think has offered the least help to his brand.

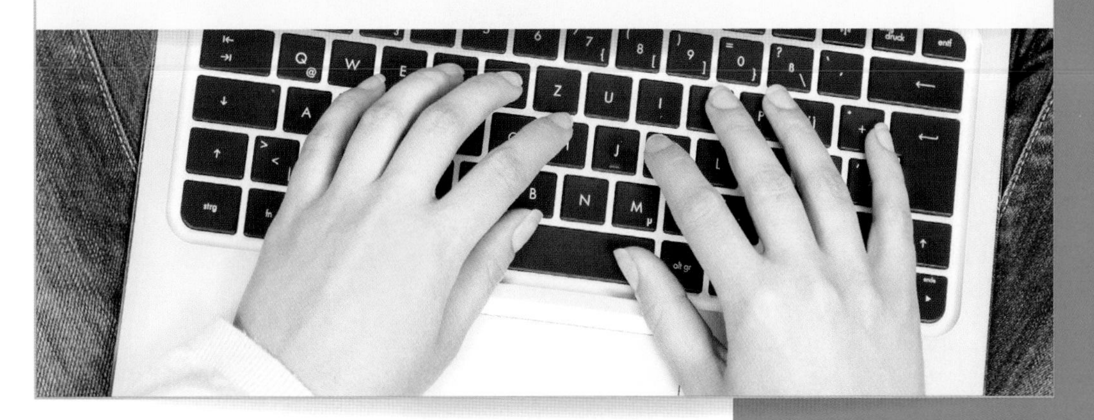

Words to Understand

ultimately: serves as a synonym for "finally" and signifies the end of something, such as a list.

faux: something that is not real or is an imitation, fake, or counterfeit; this French word is pronounced "fō."

networking: interacting with fellow professionals and other influential people in an industry, or complementary industries, to positively affect your own career.

tangible: something that can be touched, or is otherwise very permanent and real.

Chapter 4

How Drake Built a Better Brand

Drake has famously sung about starting at the bottom in building a career as one of the hottest singers in the industry. From some musicians that might sound like **faux** humility, but in Drake's case, it's absolutely true. From a relatively humble beginning, he switched professions from actor to musician and had to start his music career by creating simplistic mixtapes as the building blocks of his future success. Here, then, is a brief outline of how the man who *Started from the Bottom* **ultimately** ended up on top of the world.

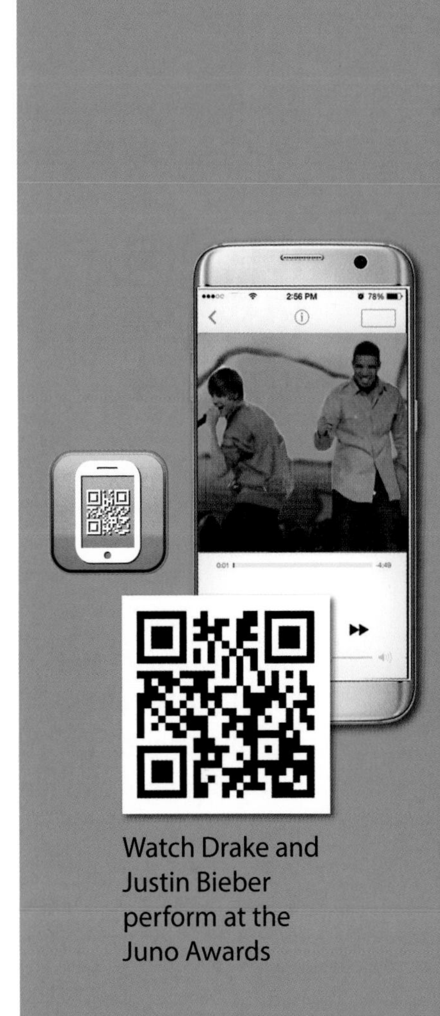

Watch Drake and Justin Bieber perform at the Juno Awards

Awards Show Performances

One way that Drake has extended his brand and built his reputation is by performing at a number of awards shows over the years, often with fellow singers he **networked** with. For instance, he performed at the April 2010 Juno Awards—highlighting excellence in Canadian music—with Justin Bieber, introducing fans of Bieber to Drake's sound as they sang a remix of Bieber's hit song *Baby*.

On February 13, 2011, he performed at the Grammy Awards with Rihanna, offering fans a live-action version of their catchy collaborative hit *What's My Name?* Drake did not win any Grammy Awards at that particular ceremony, but he was nominated for several, including Best New Artist and Best Solo Performance for *Over*.

At the BET Awards on June 26, 2011, Drake performed with Lil Wayne, Rick Ross, and DJ Khaled in a performance of DJ Khaled's *I'm On One*. This was another ceremony where Drake did not take home any awards but was nominated for several different categories, including Best Male Hip-Hop Artist and Best Collaboration for *What's My Name?* with Rihanna. Drake kept the momentum from the awards performance going that year, performing his hit song *Headlines* at the American Music Awards on November 20, 2011.

Drake and Rihanna perform at the BRIT Awards

He brought another awesome performance to the MTV Video Music Awards on August 25, 2013, playing his standout hit *Hold On, We're Going Home*. Again, he did not win the awards, but he was nominated that year for Best Hip-Hop Video and Best Direction, both for the video for *Started from the Bottom*. And on February 24, 2016, Drake performed again with Rihanna at the BRIT Awards. She was the main performer, singing her hits *Consideration* and *Work*, but Drake happily danced the night away onstage with her. At this ceremony, Drake took home the award for International Solo Male Artist.

The YOLO Years

Drake's music has been an undeniable hit, and he has also become an embedded part of pop culture in a number of ways—from creating his own brands to investing in cutting-edge businesses to becoming the very public face of music streaming for companies such as Apple Music. Additionally, he is widely credited with creating the popular phrase

"YOLO," which stands for "You Only Live Once." It came from Drake's song *The Motto*, which was released as a digital-only bonus track for his album TAKE CARE. This popular song reached the number twenty spot on *Billboard*'s Hot 100 Year-End Chart, and the song officially made this phrase the motto that the singer lives by. Even though the song came out back in 2011, "YOLO" has lived on in everything from t-shirts to hashtags, showcasing Drake's impressive ability to influence popular culture.

Another way Drake has become a permanent fixture in pop culture is through abundant internet "memes" that he has inspired. For instance, the singer had a famously goofy dance as part of his music video for the 2016 song *Hotline Bling*. Almost immediately, the internet was filled with recreations of fans imitating Drake's silly dancing, as well as remixing the music. At the time, many felt as if Drake's dancing was a joke, but the singer got the last laugh. Those silly memes and viral remixes helped increase the song's popularity and launch it to the number two spot on the *Billboard* Hot 100 Chart. The song was a hit in the United States, the UK, and around the world, which is news so good that it would make just about anybody dance!

Fast Fact 5:

Drake has also become a legend among memes by one mixing two photos of him: One shows him rejecting something and the other shows him being pleased by something. Internet users frequently use these images to humorously illustrate their likes and dislikes, particularly in pop culture.

Social Media Icon

Drake has become very adept at using different social media platforms to help him engage directly with his fans. And there are a lot of those fans! On Facebook, his page has over 35 million likes. Nearly 8

Aerial views of the areas impacted by Harvey. Photo taken on August 30, 2017

million subscribers have signed up for his YouTube channel. And on Twitter and Instagram, Drake has 36 million and 38 million followers, respectively.

In general, he uses these platforms for a mixture of "work" and "play" notifications, often tweeting about official performances and upcoming tours in between amusing personal anecdotes. When necessary, he also uses the platforms to urge his fans to make positive changes in the world, such as when he posted a video of himself imploring his fans to follow in his footsteps and donate money to the relief fund for victims of Hurricane Harvey in 2017.

OVO

One of the ways Drake has really mastered media is through "October's Very Own," better known as OVO. This name and acronym started as a humble blog where Drake reported what he and his crew had been doing. His original mixtapes were published under the unofficial OVO label. As he became more famous, OVO grew and now encompasses several different functions.

OVO Sound Radio

This program airs on *Beats 1* every couple of weeks and lets Drake to talk to his fans directly. It is also used to debut hot new music—both from Drake and up-and-coming artists.

OVO Fest

The annual concert weekend event hosted by Drake in Toronto allows him to bring hot artists to his hometown, such as Eminem, Kanye West, and Lil Wayne.

OVO Clothing

Fans can purchase official Drake swag items either online, or in the brick-and-mortar stores in Toronto, Los Angeles, or New York City. OVO Clothing has collaborated with Air Jordan and Canada Goose, as well as others, in producing baseball hats, seasonal clothing items, jackets, and more!

OVO Sound

OVO Sound is now the name of Drake's Toronto-based Canadian record label, which he runs through a partnership with Warner Bros. Records. This impressive achievement lets Drake have the best of both worlds as he reaps the benefits of his generous contract with Young Money Entertainment while using his own label to promote rising stars in the music industry.

Complex Lyrics

As a singer, Drake has walked a very fine line with his lyrics. His albums are usually considered rap or hip-hop albums, and he frequently works with rap icons like Lil Wayne. Some of his lyrics (and music videos) reinforce the idea that fame and a party lifestyle are great goals. Predominantly, though, Drake is known for his more sensitive lyrics.

Best I Ever Had

(Released February 13, 2009)

Drake famously says that when his girlfriend is hanging around the house in comfy clothes with no makeup on, she's actually more beautiful than ever. It's a sweet lyric that emphasizes how beauty should be natural—not a function of sexy clothes or lots of makeup. It's not hard to see why songs like this have cemented Drake's reputation for being emotional and romantic.

A Night Off

(Released February 13, 2009)

In *A Night Off*, he sings to his partner that he earnestly wishes he could be with her when she is feeling lonely. It's a simple sentiment, but it's also powerful: Drake embodies every romantic partner who aspires to make pain go away for the people he loves.

Over the years, these sensitive, romantic lyrics have formed the cornerstone of Drake's brand, and they are one reason why he is viewed as a rather wholesome singer, despite the raucous world of professional rap music that he lives in.

Girls Love Beyoncé

(Released April 15, 2013)

In this tune, Drake sings about how he needs someone who can help him think about other people, not just himself. The song is surprisingly introspective and showcases Drake's belief that romance is not a matter of pursuing only one's own satisfaction. Instead, he desires a romance where the other person can help to make him a better person day by day—one who is worthy of her love.

Using Public Speeches to Make Important Statements

Graduation Speech at Jarvis Collegiate Institute

In 2012, Drake famously went back to finish his studies and receive his high school diploma at the age of twenty-six. The next month, he celebrated by giving the commencement speech at Jarvis Collegiate Institute. This gave him a unique opportunity to speak to fellow graduates about his own experience of leaving school and then returning. He described a void inside himself that he felt at leaving something as important as his education incomplete.

Drake giving a 2012 commencement speech

I was one of those students that, despite the incredible support and despite the incredible knowledge and the incredible love that [they] would show me every single day, I still managed to fight this education system and say, "It wasn't for me." I wanna let you know today as I stand in front of you that, I get it. I get why this institution is in place for each and every one of us. It's not necessarily about the books that you will read or the science or the math equations that you will do because you may end up taking a path in life where the things that you have learned, you can't necessarily fully apply, and that's okay. It's not about the popular kids and the kids that don't feel as popular because all of that changes. I promise you, I'm 26 years old and all of that changes. What this is about, today, for all of you, is the art of following through, and that is one of the most important life lessons that my uncle has taught me. It's about teaching the art of following through, and I want to say that I'm so proud of you because there are different ways to follow through. Tonight you followed through with a straight shot, and for that, you should give yourself a round of applause. For me, my follow-through was different. I had to double back. I reached a point in my life where I realized that there aren't material things that could give me the excitement that I'm looking for.

There's a void, there is a gap in my life that I need to fill, and I needed to sit long and hard to think about what that was. And it was the fact that I had left a gaping hole in my story of following through ... So for five months, we talked back and forth on emails, we worked, I wrote papers, I studied for an exam, and we figured out how I could close my chapter of following through."

In many ways, this is the most inspirational speech Drake has ever given. Many people dismiss his concerns—and those of other ultra-rich celebrities—because they assume that people with that amount of wealth are not missing anything in their lives. However, Drake used his speech to highlight the idea that every person has a void inside themselves, and that money and material things are not enough to fill it. Instead, the singer presented the poetic idea of human lives as stories that we create day by day. For him, his failure to graduate high school meant leaving part of his own story unfinished. In finding what was necessary to complete his story, Drake also found something to fill the void and complete himself.

On a more **tangible** level, Drake's message on the importance of following through is one that can resonate with everyone. He correctly identifies the negative stereotypes that many people have of school and of education—for instance, that school is filled with concepts and theories that don't apply to real life, and that it is little more than a popularity contest waged by rival cliques. However, as Drake notes, this became more about building his own sense of character than about memorizing a dry theory or an abstract concept. To him, it was important to finish what he started, and walking away from an achievement that was within his grasp had filled him with years of regret.

Drake is a man that has everything he could ever want in terms of material desires, but his speech is a reminder that if we walk away from goals and dreams, we lose what we truly need in our lives.

Response to Grammy Award Controversy

While Drake has won many awards, there was one year when his achievements rubbed many fans the wrong way. This occurred when his hit song *Hotline Bling* won the Grammy Award for Best Rap Song in 2017. Fans were perplexed because the song was clearly more of a pop song, and it literally contained no rapping.

Eventually, Drake himself spoke about the award and the controversy it caused.

> *I am referred to as a black artist … I'm a black artist … I'm apparently a rapper, even though* Hotline Bling *is not a rap song. The only category they can manage to fit me in is in a rap category, maybe because I've rapped in the past or because I'm black. I can't figure out why … There's pop obligations they have, and I fluked out…*
>
> *I fluked out and got one of the biggest songs of the year that is a pop song and I'm proud of that. I love the rap world and I love the rap community … I write pop songs for a reason. I want to be like Michael Jackson. I want to be like artists that I looked up to. Those are pop songs, but I never get any credit for that … By the way, I'm speaking to you as a winner. I won two awards (last night), but I don't even want them because it just feels weird for some reason. It just doesn't feel right to me. I feel almost alienated, or like they're trying to purposely alienate me by making me win rap awards or pacify me by handing me something and putting me in that category because it's the only place where [they] can figure out where to put me.*

Oftentimes, famous musicians and other celebrities get a reputation for being out of touch with reality. However, in this blunt speech, Drake revealed that he was in agreement with many of his fans when he clarified that he too objected to the 2017 Grammy Awards that he won. Specifically, he balked at the fact that *Hotline Bling* managed to win awards for both Best Rap/Sung Performance and Best Rap Song…despite it not being a rap song!

Drake's thoughts on this issue are in line with other music artists, such as Bruno Mars, who have expressed how the color of their skin has led to music critics and executives trying to stereotype them. Broadly speaking, this refers to the darker side of the music industry as a business, and as a business, executives must choose how to market songs to particular demographics. This creates a tension between Drake's desire to have a worldwide mass appeal (like his idol, Michael Jackson) and the music industry's desire to lump all of Drake's music into traditionally black categories such as rap, even when the song is blatantly not a rap song.

It would have been very easy for Drake to get defensive about the criticism of his wins and embrace the achievement. After all, there are few awards more significant to most musicians than the Grammys. Instead, he offered a very thoughtful comment on race and American stereotyping. Drake clarified that he is proud of his music as pop music, but that he got lumped into the rap category out of some combination of racism on the part of critics and genuine confusion over what musical genre his music inhabits.

Either way, the end result is the same: Despite having critical acclaim, extreme wealth, and several high-profile awards, the intersection of race and culture, as well as racism and stereotyping, can leave anyone feeling isolated and lonely. Drake's willingness to speak out about this, though, is important because it shows his willingness to use his fame and platform to reach out toward others who may be feeling that same sense of isolation and alienation.

Text-Dependent Questions:

❶ What famous phrase is Drake credited with coining?

❷ At what institute did Drake give a stirring graduation speech?

❸ Why was Drake's Grammy Award for Best Rap Song controversial?

Research Project:

Research the origin and history of rap music. Create a list of common characteristics of a rap song: What kind of lyrics do they contain? What instruments are used in most of the songs? What types of locations do rap artists generally perform at? What themes do rap songs typically encompass?

Then research the origin and history of pop music and create the same kind of list, with the answers pertaining to pop songs.

Put the lists in front of you and listen to *Hotline Bling*. Put a check mark next to each characteristic that this song demonstrates. Which list has more check marks—rap or pop? Share your lists with your friends and see if they agree with your assessment of whether *Hotline Bling* is a rap song or a pop song.

Words to Understand

human trafficking: an organized criminal activity in which human beings are treated as possessions to be controlled and exploited, and frequently forced from one place to another and made to work involuntarily.

honorarium: special payment made for a service that was offered without any charge.

Samaritan: a word for a helpful person that derives from the biblical parable of the Good Samaritan.

Chapter 5

Supporting the Community

Caring about People and Causes

A very important quality for any famous celebrity is their ability to give back to the communities around them. After all, their careers are built on the happiness and goodwill of their fans, and such fame gives singers like Drake a unique platform to both directly donate money to various causes and to call for others to do the same. And Drake actually has a long and impressive history of donating to various causes, relief efforts, and individuals.

Most of Drake's donations to charities have been relatively quiet, but there is one charity he supports wholeheartedly.

Thorn

This organization began back in 2009 when it was founded by actors Demi Moore and Ashton Kutcher. The mission of Thorn is to prevent the exploitation of children via **human trafficking** and to help catch and prosecute criminals engaged in this activity. Their Technology Task Force works with companies all around the world to utilize technology in creative ways to protect children from online predators. Drake is one of many well-known celebrities (including others, such as actor Bradley Cooper and musician Justin Timberlake) whose donations have helped the company safeguard youngsters. Drake has been supporting this charity since 2013.

Justin Timberlake

Charity Softball

One of Drake's more unconventional charities is one that practically has his name on it! Since 2014, Drake has organized and headlined an annual event in Houston, Texas, dubbed "Houston Appreciation Week." This is an indication of how much the city means to him. This is where he met Lil Wayne, which contributed toward Drake being signed to Young Money Entertainment and launching an explosive career. Drake describes Houston as "one of the greatest places in the entire world." He uses this event to give back to the city in very creative ways.

For instance, during Houston Appreciation Week in 2015, the singer hosted a softball game at the University of Houston. As a charity event, the money raised went toward the Astros Urban Youth Academy. Drake's fame and the prospect of a week of sheer fun in Houston have attracted more celebrities and professional athletes each year. As the affair grows, Drake continues to help the city of Houston prosper.

Dixon Hall

When it comes to donating to worthy causes, Drake got started very early in his career. You might think it's easy for the "famous multimillionaire Drake" to donate money, but it's notable to see that he still did so back when he was relatively unknown.

For example, in 2011, Drake won the Allan Slaight Award for the second time. The award is intended to honor the talent of notable young Canadians—Drake describes himself as a "proud Canadian." At the tender age of twenty-four, Drake certainly qualified.

The award came with a $10,000 **honorarium**, and the young, unsigned singer could have easily taken that money for himself. Instead, he donated all of it to Dixon Hall, a special community service organization dedicated to helping low-income individuals in and around Toronto, Canada. In this way, Drake showed his commitment to helping others who, like himself, aspire to be more than their humble beginnings might indicate.

Hurricane Harvey Relief

The year 2017 was memorable because of several terrible hurricanes, including Hurricane Harvey. That storm made landfall in Texas on August 25, causing massive amounts of damage to the state. Overall, it killed eighty-nine people in the United States, caused at least $70 billion in damage, and displaced over 30,000 people. To help Texas, the state he loves so much, Drake donated $200,000 of his own money through a YouCaring.com fundraiser. It was started by J.J. Watt, a professional defensive end for the Houston Texans U.S. football team.

Drake took his donation a step further by posting a video to his popular Instagram account in which he implored his fans to donate money. In the video, Drake said,

> *To the brave men and women that have assisted in aid, relief, and rescue, your actions are truly heroic … The journey to rebuilding is going to be a long one, so anything you can give is greatly appreciated.*

This is yet another example of Drake using his popularity and his platform to make the world a better place. By September 15, 2017—less than a month after the hurricane hit—the almost 210,000 donors on YouCaring.com raised $37 million for relief aid—far above the original $20 million goal.

Drake's plea for fans to send donations to help victims of Hurricane Harvey

Strawberry Mansion High School

While most of Drake's donations have been financial in nature, Strawberry Mansion High School received a very different kind of gift. Drake first learned about the school through an ABC News Special that highlighted the level of violence the school and surrounding area had experienced. The special also emphasized how the principal, Linda Claitt-Wayman, was starting a number of initiatives to reduce violence and help her students.

Drake decided that he wanted to contribute, so he donated $75,000 to the school for a dedicated recording studio. He invited students to a concert in the area and told them,

> *This is about you. This is about your principal. This is about your future. . . I love you. I care about you. I want to see you succeed.*

Drake's contribution spearheaded donations to the school across the nation, and now, the school no longer experiences massive amounts of violence. In addition, the majority of the graduating seniors pursue college degrees.

Computer Schools in Jamaica

Interestingly, Drake's willingness to aid schools is international! Even before he assisted Strawberry Mansion High School, Drake took note of a struggling community in Kingston, Jamaica, called Cassava Piece. One of his friends, reggae artist Mavado, is from that area, and when Drake visited, he felt honored by the children of the area. He described them as running around after him wherever he went.

Drake donated $30,000 to help build computer schools in the area so that those children could have a better, brighter future. During an interview with ***Samaritan** Mag* (an online magazine dedicated to spotlighting the good deeds of others), Drake also offered some thoughtful words about his philosophy of donating money and time. For instance, he said he was happy to cover artist K'naan's song *Wavin' Flag* for charity simply because the other singer asked him to do it.

> *"Otherwise, I didn't want to get involved with anything to do with Haiti because I never want to make it feel like it's press, you know? I don't want to go searching for the look."*

Drake went on to say that the personal connection he felt to this area of Jamaica and to his friend Mavado motivated him to contribute, and that "the more causes I find that I can connect to, I'd love to be a part of." Overall, Drake is very concerned about making sure that his donations and charity work help the people who need it most—rather than simply glorifying Drake himself.

Working in Conjunction with The Game

Drake has shown a strong commitment to helping large numbers of people via his charity work and donations, but there was one amazing instance where he aided a single individual.

In September 2013, a resident of Tiffin, Ohio, experienced the unthinkable: Her boyfriend and five children all died when their mobile home caught fire. Anna Angel survived only because she was working at the time. In addition to dealing with her grief, she was struggling to pay for funerals for everybody.

This was where Drake, along with fellow musician The Game, stepped in. Together, the two singers donated $20,000 to Anna, and they convinced the reality television production company 51 Minds to donate an additional $2,250. While no amount of money could bring Anna's loved ones back, this gesture spotlighted Drake's willingness to help someone cope with the worst time in her life and also bring public attention to her plight.

Fast Fact 6:

At the time, Anna Angel worked a low-paying job at Burger King. Paying for six funerals would have been impossible without assistance. In Ohio, the National Association of Funeral Directors (NFDA) calculated the average cost of a funeral at $7,045. Multiplied by six, the charge could have been as much as $42,000. If Anna earned Ohio's 2013 minimum wage, she would have had to work over 5,000 hours—equaling two and a half years at forty hours per week—just to cover this expense.

Given that reality, Drake's act was undeniably generous. It also stood out among his charitable deeds, as he typically works through companies or charity foundations to raise money for particular causes. In this case, though, he was apparently so moved by the tragedy of this woman that he felt the need to personally contribute.

Drake's Own Struggles

It's easy to think that Drake hasn't suffered through very many struggles. After all, even before he was a multimillionaire singer, he was a famous actor. And before he was a famous actor, he was a high school student going to a prestigious school while living just outside of Forest Hill, a wealthy neighborhood of Toronto. However, Drake experienced some unique difficulties growing up, and there were other special challenges he had to overcome on his road to fame.

For example, Drake's parents divorced when he was only five years old. In addition to the usual trauma that divorce has on young children, it touched off a religious struggle for Drake. His father is a practicing Catholic, but his mother is a devout Jew. After the divorce, Drake was raised by his mother in Canada; his father moved back to Memphis, Tennessee. The future singer grew up Jewish, but this presented its own obstacles as he got older.

As an example, Drake did not always live in the more affluent sections of Toronto. They lived in Weston Road (a much more blue-collar, working-class area) before moving to Forest Hill. And the move wasn't entirely positive. In an interview with *Vibe* magazine, Drake recalled that "Jewish kids didn't understand how I could be black and Jewish." He summed up the experience of going to school at Forest Hills Collegiate Institute like this: "It was just stupid, annoying rich kids being close-minded and mean."

In some ways, the struggle has continued into adulthood. While Drake often identifies as Jewish, some of his music videos have garnered criticism that questions his stand. For instance, the music video for *HYFR* features images like the singer smoking marijuana in a synagogue. In some ways, that song and video represent Drake's essential struggle in balancing issues of faith, race, class, and public perception…all while trying to remain true to himself.

Fast Fact 7:

Drake's faith was questioned again when he mentioned talking to God in the song *Still Here*, from his album VIEWS. Praying is seen as more of a Christian activity than a Jewish one, so it caused people to wonder. Some Christian websites insisted that other songs on VIEWS were about his "faith and spirituality" and that the album dealt "with themes of faith and Christianity."

This public desire to pin down his faith, and identify where he falters in his faith, is similar to his struggles within the music industry. Once again, Drake seems to be interested in creating something dynamic and new (in this case, regarding his religious beliefs), while the industry and some in the public feel the need to shoehorn him into pre-existing categories.

As mentioned in an earlier chapter, even as an adult, Drake still has issues with people incorrectly identifying his particular brand of music. He was as perplexed as many music lovers when he won a Best Rap Song Grammy Award for *Hotline Bling*, which has no rap in it at all. He cynically mentioned on OVO Radio that he wanted to give the awards back, believing that music critics were focusing on things like previous rap songs, or even his race. For a singer who is constantly trying to move forward with his music and style, the realization that critics may never see past previous accomplishments—or even skin color—was a particularly bitter moment for Drake.

Final Thoughts

Drake is more private about his donations than other celebrities because he never wants to make the struggles that others are facing into little more than a public-relations opportunity for him. However, he has a long history of donating money to the causes and individuals he thinks have the greatest need, and he has done his best to be a force for both change and good in the world.

And, of course, all of this is shaped by his ongoing struggles. People have tried to tear him down for everything from the color of his skin to the faith in his heart. Fortunately, Drake is a role model for coping with our own challenges, showing how it is possible to emerge from them stronger than ever before.

Text-Dependent Questions:

1. Outside of the United States, where else has Drake helped fund schools?
2. What faith does Drake identify as?
3. Why did Drake contribute to a $20,000 donation to a woman in Ohio?

Research Project:

Compare Drake's different charitable donations with another popular musician's. Write about which one you think has had a more positive impact on the world and their communities. Why do you feel that way? Are there any charities or relief efforts you feel Drake should have donated to but he did not? If you had money to donate, which types of charities would you contribute to?

Series Glossary of Key Terms

A&R: an abbreviation that stands for Artists and Repertoire, which is a record company department responsible for the recruitment and development of talent; similar to a talent scout for sports.

ambient: a musical style that relies on electronic sounds, gentle music, and the lack of a regular beat to create a relaxed mood for the listener.

brand: a particular product or a characteristic that serves to identify a particular product; a brand name is one having a well-known and usually highly regarded or marketable word or phrase.

cameo: also called a cameo role; a minor part played by a prominent performer in a single scene of a motion picture or a television show.

choreography: the art of planning and arranging the movements, steps, and patterns of dancers.

collaboration: a product created by working with someone else; combining individual talents.

debut: a first public appearance on a stage, on television, or so on, or the beginning of a profession or career; the first appearance of something, like a new product.

deejay (DJ): a slang term for a person who spins vinyl records on a turntable; aka a disc jockey.

demo: a recording of a new song, or of one performed by an unknown singer or group, distributed to disc jockeys, recording companies, and the like, to demonstrate the merits of the song or performer.

dubbed: something that is named or given a new name or title; in movies, when the actors' voices have been replaced with those of different performers speaking another language; in music, transfer or copying of previously recorded audio material from one medium to another.

endorsement: money earned from a product recommendation, typically by a celebrity, athlete, or other public figure.

entrepreneur: a person who organizes and manages any enterprise, especially a business, usually with considerable initiative and at financial risk.

falsetto: a man singing in an unnaturally high voice, accomplished by creating a vibration at the very edge of the vocal chords.

genre: a subgroup or category within a classification, typically associated with works of art, such as music or literature.

hone, honing: sharpening or refining a set of skills necessary to achieve success or perform a specific task.

icon: a symbol that represents something, such as a team, a religious person, a location, or an idea.

innovation: the introduction of something new or different; a brand-new feature or upgrade to an existing idea, method, or item.

instrumental: serving as a crucial means, agent, or tool; of, relating to, or done with an instrument or tool.

jingle: a short verse, tune, or slogan used in advertising to make a product easily remembered.

mogul: someone considered to be very important, powerful, and in charge; a term usually associated with heads of businesses in the television, movie studio, or recording industries.

performing arts: skills that require public performance, as acting, singing, or dancing.

philanthropy: goodwill to fellow members of the human race; an active effort to promote human welfare.

public relations: the activity or job of providing information about a particular person or organization to the public so that people will regard that person or organization in a favorable way.

sampler: a digital or electronic musical instrument, related to a synthesizer, that uses samples, or sound recordings, of real instruments (trumpet, violin, piano, etc.) mixed with excerpts of recorded songs and other interesting sounds (sirens, ocean waves, construction noises, car horns, etc.) that are stored digitally and can be replayed by a triggering device, like a sequencer, electronic drums, or a MIDI keyboard.

single: a music recording having two or more tracks that is shorter than an album, EP, or LP; also, a song that is particularly popular, independent of other songs on the same album or by the same artist.

Further Reading

Drake: An Unauthorized Biography. Waukegan: Belmont and Belcourt Biographies, 2012.

Emerson, Rock. *"You Can Thank Me Now": The Biography of Aubrey "Drake" Graham.* New York: Knice House Publishing, 2011.

Kennedy, Robert. *Drake.* New York: Gareth Stevens Publishing, 2012.

Orr, Tamra. *Drake.* Kennett Square: Purple Toad Publishing, 2014.

Peppas, Lynn. *Drake.* New York: Crabtree Publishing, 2011.

Internet Resources

www.drakeofficial.com
Drake's official website.

www.facebook.com/Drake
Drake's official Facebook page.

www.youtube.com/user/DrakeOfficial
Drake's official YouTube channel.

www.billboard.com/
Official Billboard Music website.

twitter.com/drake?lang=en
Drake's official Twitter account.

Citations

"Kicked off the show..." by Drake. "Drake Explains Why He Was 'Kicked Off' Degrassi." Interview by Andres Tardio. MTV News. October 15, 2015.

"One of the greatest feelings..." by Drake. Twitter post. October 17, 2012.

"The campaign is really about creativity..." by Drake. "Drake Teams with Sprite for 'Spark' Campaign." Interview by Mariel Concepion. *Billboard*. February 11, 2010.

"Realest dude ever..." by Drake. Alison Millington. "How Drake and an Ex-Banker Created a Luxury Whiskey That Looks Like High-End Champagne and is hot on Instagram." *Business Insider*. July 19, 2017.

"Cultural moments," by Zane Lowe. "Exclusive: How Drake and Apple Music Broke Streaming Records with More Life." Interview by Micah Singleton. *The Verge*. March 25, 2017.

"15,000 people," by Jas Prince. "The Untold Story of How Drake Met Lil Wayne." Interview by Zara Golden. *The Fader*. June 11, 2015.

"I was one of those students..." by Drake. "Drake Gives Inspiring Graduation Speech to Grads of Jarvis Collegiate Institute." Betty Bema Simpson. AXS. October 09, 2012.

"I am referred to as a black artist..." by Drake. "Drake Doesn't Think He Deserved to Win at the 2017 Grammys, 'I Don't Even Want Them.'" JustJared.com. February 19, 2017.

"One of the greatest places..." by Drake. "Drake Makes a Hit with Charity Softball Event." Alyson Footer. *MLB News*. May 22, 2015.

"Proud Canadian," by Drake. "Drake Wins Award, Gives Cash to Charity." *The Toronto Star*. August 16, 2011.

"To the brave men and women..." by Drake. "Drake Donates $200,000 to Hurricane Harvey Relief Efforts." Carl Lamarre. *Billboard*. August 31, 2017.

"This is about you..." by Drake. "Drake Donates $75,000 to Help Open Philadelphia High School Music Studio." Will Robinson. EW.com. March 11, 2015.

"Otherwise, I don't want to get involved..." by Drake. "Drake Donates $30,000 to Build Computer Schools In Jamaica." Interview by Karen Bliss. *Samaritan Mag*. April 27, 2010.

"Jewish kids didn't understand..." by Drake. "Drake Covers *Vibe* Magazine's 'Race Issue.'" BET.com. December 19, 2013.

"...faith and spirituality..." Christian Deguit. "Drake samples Christian Song in New Track 'Views'; Raps about Faith and Spirituality in New Album." ChristianDaily.com. May 23, 2016.

"...with themes of faith and Christianity." Deguit, "Drake Samples..." ChristianDaily.com.

Educational Videos

Chapter 1:
http://x-qr.net/1H2C
http://x-qr.net/1FJd
http://x-qr.net/1GzU
http://x-qr.net/1FwE
http://x-qr.net/1HrX
http://x-qr.net/1EgL
http://x-qr.net/1Gc9

Chapter 2:
http://x-qr.net/1DcU

Chapter 3:
http://x-qr.net/1H55
http://x-qr.net/1Ddi
http://x-qr.net/1F9M
http://x-qr.net/1HJZ
http://x-qr.net/1HQS
http://x-qr.net/1Eeo
http://x-qr.net/1FCf

Chapter 4:
http://x-qr.net/1ESR
http://x-qr.net/1GPn
http://x-qr.net/1FUo

Chapter 5:
http://x-qr.net/1Exn

Photo Credits

Chapter 1:
Rapper Drake performing in 2017 in Toronto.png | Wikimedia Commons © Shot by Drew: Drake (The Come Up Show)
Drake-August-2017.jpg | Wikimedia Commons
Drake_at_the_Velvet_Underground_-_2017_(36398066420).jpg | Wikimedia Commons
ID 24036834 © Carrienelson1 | Dreamstime
ID 24617824 © Sbukley | Dreamstime
ID 30010694 © Sbukley | Dreamstime
ID 37287829 © Sbukley | Dreamstime
ID 53895810 © Starstock | Dreamstime
ID 99079886 © Starstock | Dreamstime

Chapter 2:
Drake-2017.png | © flickr
Drake_fox_theatre.jpg | © Karla Moy - hustlegrl.com
Drake_at_Bun-B_Concert_2011-_The_Come_Up_Show.jpg | Wikimedia Commons © Shot by Drew: Drake (The Come Up Show)
ID 24036835 © Carrienelson1 | Dreamstime
ID 37717088 © Bigapplestock | Dreamstime

Chapter 3:
Organik_and_drake.jpg | © MrShamrock | Wikimedia Commons
ID 27559790 © Roystudio | Dreamstime
ID 34073910 © Little_prince | Dreamstime
ID 35296249 © Ivan Mikhaylov | Dreamstime
ID 31737905 © Sbukley | Dreamstime
ID 42235228 © Creativeimpression | Dreamstime
ID 47646040 © Dwong19 | Dreamstime
ID 48118024 © Jaguarps | Dreamstime
ID 76690836 © Natthapon Ngamnithiporn | Dreamstime

Chapter 4:
ID 13917470 © Kristinashu | Dreamstime
ID 101211027 © Karl Spencer | Dreamstime
ID 30012692 © Sbukley | Dreamstime
ID 25959170 © Sbukley | Dreamstime

Chapter 5:
ID 38421348 © Pixelrobot | Dreamstime
ID 34828227 © Featureflash | Dreamstime
ID 58880394 © Bobby17 | Dreamstime

Index

Index

Index

Author's Biography

Chris Snellgrove received a PhD in English from Auburn University in 2012. In addition to publishing several academic texts and educational materials, he is a veteran online writer for websites such as Listverse, Grunge, Looper, and Screenrant. His academic specialty was American literature, but his later interest (in terms of both academic and freelance writing) has been pop culture. He has spoken at academic conferences through America and currently serves as an assistant professor of English at Northwest Florida State College in Niceville, Florida, and he lives in Crestview, Florida, with his wife, son, and two dogs.